Wide Range
Starters
Green Book 1

Phyllis Flowerdew

Oliver & Boyd

Acknowledgment

'The Fruit Tree' was adapted, with permission, from a story called 'The Famine and the Fruit Tree' in *Where The Leopard Passes* by Geraldine Elliot (© Geraldine Elliot 1949), published by Routledge & Kagan Paul Ltd.

Illustrated by Leonora Box, Nancy Bryce, Tamasin Cole, Maggie Ling and Dave Simmonds

Oliver & Boyd
Robert Stevenson House
1–3 Baxter's Place
Leith Walk
Edinburgh EH1 3BB

A Division of Longman Group Ltd

First published 1985
Second impression 1986

© Phyllis Flowerdew 1985
All rights reserved. No part of this publication may be reproduced, stored in a retrieval system, or transmitted in any form or by any means, electronic, mechanical, photocopying, recording or otherwise, without the prior written permission of the Publishers.

ISBN 0 05 003687 4

Set in 16/24 point Monophoto Plantin
Produced by Longman Group (FE) Ltd
Printed in Hong Kong

Where to find the Stories

Page

- 4   The Car That Spoke
- 14   The Pool of the Moon
- 24   The Runaway Pram
- 34   The Fruit Tree
- 41   The Post Office Cat

The Car that Spoke

Mrs Long bought a car
at the garage
and drove it away.
It was a second-hand car
but it went very well.

Mrs Long drove along the road.

She passed houses.

She passed fields.

She passed trees.

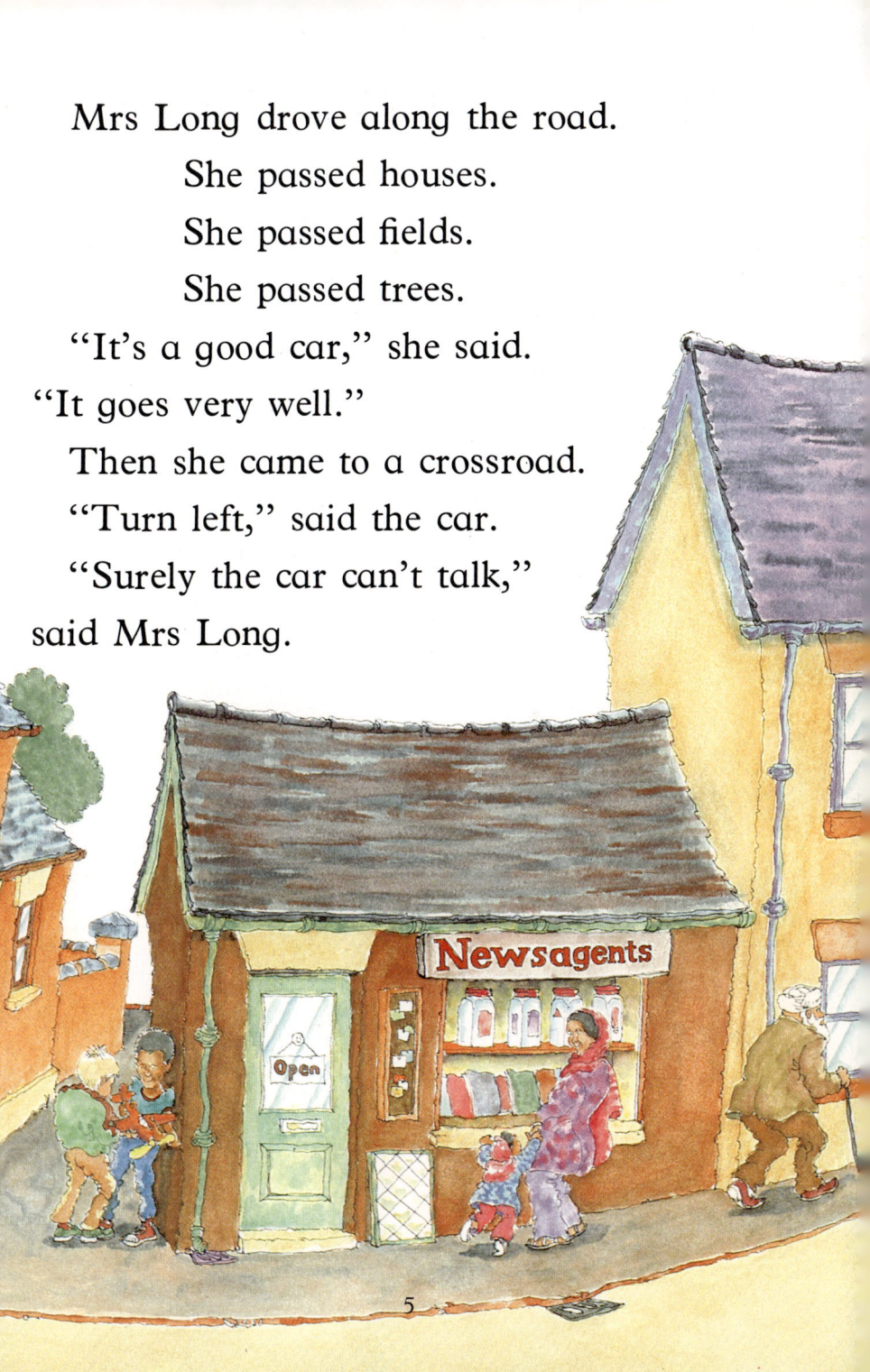

"It's a good car," she said. "It goes very well."

Then she came to a crossroad.

"Turn left," said the car.

"Surely the car can't talk," said Mrs Long.

"Turn left," said the car again.

"I don't want to turn left," said Mrs Long.

All the same, she did turn left just to keep the car quiet.

Then she drove on.

    She passed houses.

    She passed fields.

    She passed trees.

Soon she came to another crossroad.

"Turn left," said the car.

"I don't want to turn left," said Mrs Long.

"Turn left," said the car again.
So Mrs Long did turn left,
just to keep the car quiet.

Then she drove on.

She passed houses.

She passed fields.

She passed trees.

Soon the car came to another crossroad.

"Turn left," said the car.

Mrs Long was feeling very angry now.

"I don't WANT to turn left," she said,
"and I don't want a car
that tells me what to do."

"Turn left," said the car again.

"I will not," said Mrs Long.

"I don't WANT to turn left."

"If I turn left here,
I shall come to a place
where a stream crosses the road."

"Turn left," said the car.

"I will NOT," said Mrs Long,
but two other cars
were waiting behind her,
and they were hooting and hooting,
so poor Mrs Long
did turn left after all.

There had been a lot of rain that week,
and there was more water
in the stream than usual.
Mrs Long's car splashed through it.
Then in the very middle, it stopped.

"Go on," said Mrs Long,
but the car couldn't move.

Some boys were playing by the stream.
They splashed into the water
and pushed the car to the other side,
and it started up again.

"Thank you," said Mrs Long.

Then as she drove along the road,
she said to herself,

"I shall take the car
back to the garage,
and ask the man to change it.
I don't want a car
that tells me what to do."

But just then
she came to a crossroad.
She waited for the car to say,
"Turn left,"
but it didn't speak.
It didn't make a sound.

"Aha," said Mrs Long,
"perhaps you left your voice
in the stream.
Perhaps the water got into your engine."

Then she drove on along the road.
She passed houses.
She passed fields.
She passed trees.
The car went very well,

and it didn't speak at all.

"It's a good car," said Mrs Long.
"It's a good car
now that it doesn't tell me
what to do."

By the time
she reached the garage,
she was very pleased
with the car,
and she didn't want
to change it after all.

But she did go inside
and say to the garage man,
"Who had this car
before I bought it?"

"An inventor,"
said the garage man.
"He was always inventing things
and making things,
but they didn't always work properly.'

"Oh," said Mrs Long.
"Now I know."

The Pool of the Moon

There was once a pool of clear fresh water. It was called "The Pool of the Moon", because sometimes the moon shone right over it, and looked as if it were floating on the water.

A family of hares lived near by,
and every day
they went to the pool to drink.
Their paws were so small
and their noses were so soft
that they made not a ripple
in the still water.
  Then one summer
a herd of elephants
came that way.
They found The Pool of the Moon,

and began to drink from it.
   Their big feet
and their long trunks
sent ripples running
across the water.
   Their big feet
and their long trunks
stirred up the mud
at the bottom of the pool.

Some of the elephants
even trod on some of the hares
and hurt them.
The hares felt very angry.
"The elephants are spoiling our pool,"
they said.
"Perhaps they will not come again,"
said the biggest hare.
But they did.
They came every day.
Every day their big feet
and their long trunks
sent ripples running
across the water.

Every day their big feet
and their long trunks
stirred up the mud
at the bottom of the pool.

Every day some of the elephants
even trod on some of the hares
and hurt them.

"How can we stop the elephants?"
said the hares.
"They are so big
and we are so small."

"I have an idea,"
said the biggest hare.
"Next week the moon will be shining
over the pool.
It will look
as if it is floating
on the water.
When the elephants come to drink,
their big feet and their long trunks
will send ripples running
across the water.
The ripples will make it look
as if the moon is shaking with anger.

I will go to the elephants
and tell them
that the moon is angry with them."

So a few days later,
the biggest hare
went to the elephants.

"The moon is angry with you
because you are spoiling our pool,"
he said.

The elephants did not believe
that the moon was angry,
so they went on
going to the pool to drink
as usual.

Then a few days later,
they saw that the moon shone
right over the pool,
and looked as if it were floating
on the water.

The elephants felt a little afraid,
but they began to drink as usual.
Their big feet
and their long trunks
sent ripples running
across the water.

At once, the moon in the water
began to shake
    and shiver
    and tremble
    and rock
    and sway.

"The hares must have spoken the truth," said the elephants.
"The moon is shaking with anger. We had better go away."

So the elephants hurried away as fast as they could go.

They never came again
to The Pool of the Moon,
so the hares were left alone
to live in peace,
and to drink
from the clear fresh water.

Adapted

The Runaway Pram

The greengrocer's shop
was at the top of the hill.
Outside it, on a wooden stand,
were oranges, bananas, apples
and some big yellow melons.

Suzy's mum was inside the shop.
Suzy was waiting outside,
holding the handle
of her baby brother's pram.

Along came two dogs,
running, playing, barking.
One dog bumped into the stand,
and sent some oranges
and big yellow melons
rolling to the ground
and down the hill.

The other dog
jumped up at Suzy
and knocked her over.
She wasn't hurt
and she got up quickly.
But oh dear!
The pram!
The pram had gone
running down the hill
all by itself,
with oranges
and big yellow melons
rolling along beside it.

The baby didn't mind.
He was sitting up,
laughing and shouting.
He thought it was fun.

"Stop the pram!" cried Suzy
to anyone who could hear.
"Please stop the pram!"

She ran down the hill after it.
She ran and ran
but she couldn't catch it.

It went on running down the hill
with oranges
and big yellow melons
rolling along beside it.

A little boy came along.
He saw the pram
running down the hill
all by itself.
He saw the baby sitting up,
laughing and shouting.

"Stop the pram!" cried the boy
to anyone who could hear,
"Please stop the pram!"

He ran down the hill after it.
He ran and ran,
but he couldn't catch it.

It went on running down the hill
with oranges
and big yellow melons
rolling along beside it.

An old lady came along.
She saw the pram
running down the hill
all by itself.
She saw the baby sitting up,
laughing and shouting.

"Stop the pram!" cried the old lady
to anyone who could hear.
"Please stop the pram!"

She ran down the hill after it.
She ran and ran
but she couldn't catch it.

It went on running down the hill
with oranges
and big yellow melons
rolling along beside it.
Then a policeman came along.
He saw the pram
running down the hill
all by itself.

He saw the oranges
and the big yellow melons
rolling along beside it.
He saw the baby sitting up,
laughing and shouting.

He saw Suzy
and the little boy
and the old lady
running behind it.

He heard everyone shouting,
"Stop the pram!
Please stop the pram!"

The policeman could run fast.
He took six great big strides
and caught hold of the pram
just as it was
about to tip over.

Then everyone stood still, puffing and blowing.

"Thank you, thank you," said Suzy,
but the baby began to cry because his fun had ended.

And the oranges
and the big yellow melons
went on rolling and rolling
and rolling
to the very bottom of the hill.

The Fruit Tree

There had been no rain
for a long, long time.
The land was very dry
and the grass had died.
The animals had almost nothing to eat.

But there was one tree
that was full of fruit.
The fruit was nearly ripe,
and it looked juicy and sweet.

But would it be good to eat?
None of the animals knew.

"How can we find out?" said the elephant.

"One of us can go to the Wise Old Snake who lives by the lake," said the tortoise. "He will know the name of the tree. He will know if the fruit is good to eat."

"That's a good idea,"
said the other animals,
"but who will go?"

"I will," said the tortoise.

"Oh no," said everyone.
"You are so slow.
You will take too long."

So the deer went instead.

He found the Wise Old Snake
who lived by the lake,
and he asked him the name of the tree.

"It is called the Mungo Mungo tree,"
said the Wise Old Snake,
"and the fruit is very good to eat."

"Thank you," said the deer,
and he ran back home.

"What is the name of the tree?"
the other animals asked him,
"and is the fruit good to eat?"

"Oh, I have forgotten already,"
said the deer.

The animals felt very cross with him.

"Someone else will have to go,"
they said.

"I will go," said the tortoise.

"Oh no," said everyone.
"You are so slow.
You will take too long."

So the elephant went instead.
He found the Wise Old Snake
who lived by the lake,
and he asked him the
name of the tree.

"It is called the Mungo Mungo tree,"
said the Wise Old Snake,
"and the fruit is very good to eat."

"Thank you," said the elephant,
and he ran back home.

"What is the name of the tree?"
the other animals asked him,
"and is the fruit good to eat?"

"Oh dear!" said the elephant.
"I have forgotten already."

The animals felt very cross with him.

"Someone else will have to go," they said.

"I will go," said the tortoise, and this time the animals said,

"Yes. Let tortoise go."

So the tortoise went.
He found the Wise Old Snake who lived by the lake, and he asked him the name of the tree.

"It is called the Mungo Mungo tree," said the Wise Old Snake, "and the fruit is very good to eat."

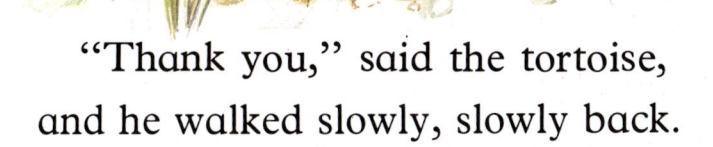

"Thank you," said the tortoise, and he walked slowly, slowly back.

By the time he reached home,
the fruit was falling to the ground,
and the animals were looking at it
and feeling very, very hungry.

Then they saw the tired little tortoise.

"What is the name of the tree?"
they asked him,
"and is the fruit good to eat?"

"It is called the Mungo Mungo tree,"
said the tortoise,
"and the fruit is very good to eat."

"Good little tortoise," they said.
"Good, clever little tortoise."
And they all began to eat
the ripe, juicy fruit at last.

Adapted

The Post Office Cat

It was a big post office
in Scotland,
and it had four cats
to keep the mice away.
The cats were half wild
and they had crept in
from the park, long ago.

Mr Mack was a sorter.
He sorted letters
into boxes and sacks.
Each box had the name of a town on it.

Mr Mack was very fond
of one of the cats.
He called it Tiger
because it had
stripy brown and yellow fur,
a bit like a tiger.

Tiger was very fond
of Mr Mack too.
She rubbed herself
against his legs
when he came to work
in the mornings.
She purred and purred
when he tickled and stroked her.
She often sat near to him
when he sorted his letters.

Then one afternoon
Tiger crept into a sack
that was lying open
on the floor.
It was full of letters
that were going to London.

It was warm in the sack
among the letters,
and soon Tiger fell fast asleep.

Sorting Office

Parcels ▶

Not long afterwards
Mr Mack tied up
the top of the sack.
Tiger was still in the sack,
lying among the letters,
fast asleep.

Mr Mack took the sack
to the place where the other sacks
were waiting to be taken
to the train.

The sacks were put
into a red post office van,
and taken to the station.

Tiger was still in the sack,
lying among the letters,
fast asleep.

When the van came to the station,
the sacks were lifted out
and put into the train
for London.

Tiger was still in the sack,
lying among the letters,
fast asleep.

The doors were closed,
and the train started on its way
to London,
jogging and jogging on the rails
through the night.

Tiger was still in the sack,
lying among the letters,
fast asleep.

Early in the morning
the train drove into London.
The doors were opened.
The sacks of letters were lifted out,
put into a red post office van
and taken to a big post office.

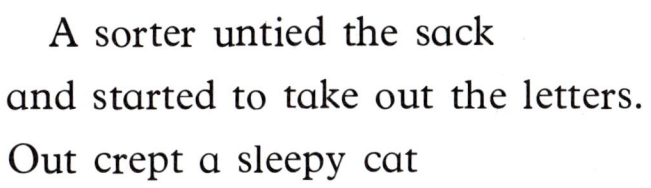

A sorter untied the sack
and started to take out the letters.
Out crept a sleepy cat
with stripy brown and yellow fur,
a bit like a tiger.

LONDON – EDINBURGH

She looked round for Mr Mack,
but Mr Mack wasn't there.

London

Tiger was puzzled.
She didn't know where she was.
She didn't know
she had been in a van
and on a train
and in another van.
She didn't know she was in London.

"You're a funny letter,"
said the sorter.
"You must have come
all the way from Scotland.
There will be a parcel van
going there later this morning.
I'll send you back in that."

So the kind man
gave Tiger some milk,
tied a label round her neck
and sent her all the way
back to Scotland
in the parcel van.

And the next day
when Mr Mack went to work
he found Tiger, the post office cat,
waiting for him as usual.